Ardmore

AN AFRICAN DISCOVERY

*

GILLIAN SCOTT

PHOTOGRAPHS BY ANTHONY BANNISTER

AND KATHLEEN COMFORT

FERNWOOD
PRESS

THE SPONSOR

The publisher gratefully acknowledges
the generous support of the principal
sponsor of this book

PUBLISHER'S ACKNOWLEDGMENTS

The publisher acknowledges with gratitude the kind
assistance of the following individuals who contributed
toward the preparation of this volume: Eleanor Kasrils,
who initiated the idea and nurtured the project until its
completion; Dr Marion Arnold, who offered considerable
insight into both the manuscript and the art of Ardmore;
and Doreen Hemp and Peter Visser for permission to
reproduce their photographs here.

AUTHOR'S ACKNOWLEDGMENTS

It was indeed a pleasure to have been afforded the
opportunity to interview the artists at Ardmore. I thank
them most sincerely for their frank replies, so accurately
translated for me by Bonnie Ntshalintshali and Moses
Nqubuka. Fée Halsted-Berning provided a wealth of
information, and was always willing to answer my many
probing questions. It was Grant Scott who suggested I
tackle this project and I am most grateful to him. Thank
you, too, to my daughter Fiona for patiently putting up
with dull weekends while I worked on the manuscript.
These and many other individuals helped make this
project possible.

FOREWORD

This celebration of the artists residing in the foothills of the Drakensberg is a tribute to the skill of the sculptors and painters at work in rural KwaZulu-Natal as well as to their artistic creativity in the best of African tradition.

In these fine examples of craft is the spontaneous and distinctly natural expression of feeling and emotion that is associated with pastoral life – marrying as it does fine art with tradition and custom, myth and legend. The pieces explode with vibrant colour and depict the artists' uncanny observations of the people, the flora and the fauna of our country.

In true South African rural tradition, most of the pieces are a social enterprise where the end product cannot truly be claimed as the work of one individual. One artist throws, another paints, and yet another glazes – each contributing his or her artistic talent to the work. Together they combine a rich, rustic appearance with a unique perspective of a modern world.

The remarkable story of the artists and their mentor and promoter represents the best of partnerships working towards transformation in our country. Their interaction has brought out the most admirable qualities of both character and art, while also heralding the arrival of local artists on the international arts agenda.

It is very pleasing that these exceptional talents, which would otherwise have withered unseen in the wilderness, have since emerged to become significant contributors to contemporary South African arts and culture.

mz mbeki

ZANELE MBEKI

Introduction

The dramatic landscape of the Barrier of Spears, as the Drakensberg is known to the Zulu people of KwaZulu-Natal, provides an imposing backdrop to the simple, greystone stables that have been converted into the Ardmore Ceramic Art Studio. The name Ardmore is taken from the farm on which Fée Halsted-Berning settled with her husband, James, in 1985. The purchase of Ardmore had brought with it not only the land, but also inherited labour tenancy relationships. Surrounded by his cattle, goats and the few horses he grazed on the land, Gwen Ntshalintshali presided over an *umuzi*, or home-stead, on Ardmore. He secured the position of *induna*, or farm headman, for himself and was quick to find domestic work for his wife, Janet, in the new farmer's home. These circumstances not only established a symbiotic relation-ship for the Ntshalintshali family, but unique employment opportunities for African people living beyond the farm.

The crisp freshness of the mountain air and the brilliant green of summer belie the harsh agricultural conditions of the area. The northeastern boundary of Ardmore rises to a high point beyond which, unseen, lie Drakensberg Location No 2 and Ntabamhlope Location, densely populated by small-scale peasant and subsis-tence farmers along the length of the Injesuthi River Valley. It is not an easy place in which to earn a living either as a commercial or subsistence farmer, and the dry, cold, brown landscape of winter presents a truer picture of agricultural prospects.

The rural experience contrasts markedly with that of township life and the urban landscape. Rural poverty is a harsh reality; those left behind by migrant workers depend on the sporadic income generated by family members working in the city or on farms, and this reality helped to shape Ardmore. The people who work at

OPPOSITE: The dry winter landscape of the scenic Champagne Valley in KwaZulu-Natal which is home to the Ardmore Studio.

ABOVE: The pastoral setting of Ardmore offers a tranquil environment which is conducive to the concentration demanded for detailed work.

Ardmore perceive their participation in the Studio first and foremost as a job. It provides them with both work and money, and this is more important than Western aesthetics associated with concepts of 'the artist'. The art of Ardmore is not driven by greater issues and those who work in the Studio know only their rural heritage and traditional background.

From the Studio, there is little sign of the location tucked away on the other side of the hill, but many of the Studio artists live there and walk for kilometres to and from work every day. Some people are fortunate enough to have land on which to grow mealies and have cows to milk, but life in the locations is difficult: the crude shelters are crowded, theft is common, and many people are unemployed and are unable to support their children. It is especially demanding for women who have no husbands. It is from this abject rural poverty that the Studio draws its artists: faced with earning a living, their primary focus is on improving the material conditions of themselves and their families.

THE STUDIO

Although the 3 377-metre buttress of Champagne Castle forms the highest point of the mountains behind the Studio, Cathkin Peak seems to loom even larger above Ardmore, like a paper cutout clearly outlined against the sky. In the winter the tawny-coloured foothills covered with thatching grass are transformed to pink, mauve and purple as the sun sets and the dark, cold night descends on the valleys, the gentle sounds reverberating across the quiet of this stark, rural landscape.

Clear blue morning skies stretch to infinity, contrasting with the yellow, orange and amber leaves of the plane tree alongside the farmstead, now used as a bed-and-

LEFT: Unlike many of the other families in the impoverished community, the Ntshalintshalis have their own livestock and farm on a small portion of the land at Ardmore.
OPPOSITE: For many of the artists, working at Ardmore has allowed them to escape arduous manual labour on local farms.

breakfast. Orange and lemon trees leading up the path to the Studio indicate some protection against the biting frost common to other parts of the KwaZulu-Natal interior. The summer landscape is transformed by a kaleidoscope of greens and, by the end of a stifling day, the mountains are often hidden by the huge, cauliflower heads of thunderstorm clouds. However, be it winter or summer, the sun is well up before the chunky doors to the old stables are opened to let in the light.

Every morning the women chatter and laugh loudly to each other as they walk down from the foothills to the Studio with their favourite paint brush protruding jauntily from their hair and, occasionally, with a sculpture balanced delicately but confidently on a head. The first person to open the door tunes in to Radio Zulu. There is a general hum as greetings are exchanged, the studio is dusted, and the work inspected before the artists settle down to their work tables in the summer, or on the grassed verges in the sun in the dry winter months. The women chat throughout the day about their personal concerns and problems, about their husbands and boyfriends and how they are cared for by them.

The driving force behind Ardmore is Fée Halsted-Berning. Trained at the Department of Fine Arts of the University of Natal, Pietermaritzburg, she majored in painting and ceramics and it was at this time that Fée encountered David Middlebrook, a visiting American lecturer who was to have a significant influence over her approach to ceramic art. Middlebrook, who sculpted in clay and marble, challenged the convention that had defined the Department's approach to ceramics, namely that clay should be used to construct relatively small, glazed, functional artefacts. For Middlebrook, clay was merely an art medium. He freed Fée from the idea that

forms should be related to kiln size, believing that the artist should control the size of the object being created and, if a piece broke, it could be repaired, an idea which is considered sacrilegious by most traditional ceramists. David Middlebrook also taught Fée that shoe polish could be used as a legitimate substitute for a glaze finish. And so Fée started sculpting and experimenting with glue and glazes, and with remoulding and reworking clay pieces. Her approach to clay and ceramics was to play a significant role in the way the Studio developed.

Fée also learnt practical lessons from Middlebrook: how to pack and set up exhibitions, manage finances, and sell works of art. Her practical experience grew after she left university in 1983 and began working with the potter David Walters in his Caversham Mill Studio in the KwaZulu-Natal Midlands. It was here that she learnt how to manage a studio and discovered that artists need

not market their work exclusively through commercial galleries, but could sell from home.

Once established at Ardmore Farm, Fée found that the isolation of the Drakensberg mountains and the lifestyle of the farming community enabled her to pursue her own creative interests. The distance from suppliers and sources of expertise meant that energy and deter-mination were required to establish a small ceramic studio on the farm. A small thatched outbuilding, with a fireplace and wall painted by an Italian prisoner of war, was the first picturesque setting for Ardmore Ceramics.

The farm brought Fée into close contact with the elements and local fauna and flora, and these features are most discernible in the organic ceramic style that characterises Ardmore works. They also pay homage to ceramic and artistic traditions associated with European art history and Western functional ceramics, notably

ABOVE: This relief, The Old Cottage Studio, *was created by Fée Halsted-Berning in 1990 and features herself and Bonnie Ntshalintshali alongside the old fireplace built by an Italian prisoner of war, Luzio Ricci, in 1914.*

the figurines and flatware produced by early English ceramic studios and factories such as Staffordshire, Worcester, Doulton and Minton.

Fée's own ceramic work fused pictorial and sculptural traditions. Born and raised in Zimbabwe, Fée Halsted-Berning's evocative images are derived from icons, photographs and objects of her Zimbabwean childhood and colonial past. She continues to collect diverse objects – Batonka stools, West African masks, Persian carpets, English china, enamel pillboxes, and Zulu bead-work – and incorporates them into her living space where they form part of her inspirational repertoire. She is also fascinated by the art and craft associated with rural lifestyle, folklore and tradition, and the whimsical yet functional pieces used in farmsteads amuse her.

These influences, combined with her African roots and a keen appreciation of the creativity of traditional wood, bead and clay work, led to the formation of her eclectic creative identity, and the famed Ardmore style was to develop from this fusion of origins.

One further influence shaped the distinct character of Ardmore ceramics: Fée had studied painting and, as a ceramic sculptor, she did not confine herself to the spectrum of colours which are usually associated with clay traditions or sculpture; her clay artefacts were concerned not only with form but also with vivid colour that imbued the work with decorative vitality.

Once she had moved to Ardmore, Fée found that she missed the stimulation and interaction with the art students that teaching had given her, and she was lonely working in the studio where she was unable to share her knowledge and expertise. And so it was that Fée asked Janet Ntshalintshali to find someone who would be willing to learn the fundamentals of ceramic art. Janet's daughter,

ABOVE: Her success as an artist has meant that Bonnie has been able to assist her father, Gwen, to support the family. The income she earns from the Studio has enabled them to substantially improve their standard of living.

Bonakele, had contracted polio as a child and found her work as a tomato picker and mealie gleaner physically arduous. Janet was therefore anxious to find work which was less strenuous for her frail daughter and this was the opportunity she had been seeking. And thus, in 1985, Bonnie Ntshalintshali started working with Fée Halsted-Berning. Bonnie's first experiments with clay were to lead to the start of an exceptional relationship.

In the Studio, Bonnie gradually forged her own idiom and style. She has a strong sense of both colour and decoration, and pays close attention to the finest details of design and texture. Her first sculptures reflected the influence of her Catholic schooling and faith. She carefully reinterpreted biblical narratives, but also incorporated traditional African rituals and references to Western consumerism in her meticulously ordered sculptural forms and painted surfaces.

Bonnie Ntshalintshali has won many awards. Her work is represented in every major public art collection in South Africa and ardent collectors of Ardmore ceramics dream of possessing something made and painted by her. As a role model, she inspires the other artists, and she retains her position of prominence in the Studio. Her colleagues who model functional ware — as opposed to the ceramic sculpture — allow her to choose the pieces she would most like to decorate before they select their own pieces to paint.

The Ardmore story was given impetus in 1990 when Fée and Bonnie won the nationally acclaimed Standard Bank Young Artist Award for Visual Art. They are the only ceramic artists thus far to have won this prestigious award. The Young Artist Award is unusual in that it is given in recognition of emerging talent, not for the production of a single piece, and the winner is required

to produce an exhibition that opens at the Standard Bank National Arts Festival in Grahamstown, and then tours to major galleries throughout South Africa. It has been important in promoting careers and introducing artists to a wide public. Fée and Bonnie are also the only artists to whom the award has been made jointly. This was in recognition of the interaction between the two artists and their mutual working environment. The award came at a time when the South African art world was concerned with the social and cultural history of the country, with fusions between different practices and concepts, and with different responses to the issue of African identity and colonial experience.

The Standard Bank Young Artist Award, and the media coverage that followed the exhibition as it toured the country, put Ardmore firmly on the map. Many awards and accolades were to follow, all of which enhanced the reputation of the Studio. In 1993, Bonnie received an invitation to participate in the Venice Biennale and her ceramic sculpture, *The Judgement*, produced for the theme 'Apocalypse', was shown at the Aperto in Venice.

In 1994, The 1820 Settlers Monument building in Grahamstown was devastated by fire but one of Bonnie's favourite sculptures, *The Nativity* – which had been purchased by The Grahamstown Foundation – survived, devoid of its paint, with a new patina of fire and smoke. The Phoenix Foundation, which was responsible for the reconstruction of the Monument, commissioned Bonnie to create a sculpture as a symbol of hope and she produced *The Resurrection*.

As the Ardmore Studio grew in popularity, so it grew in size. More space was required and the greystone horse stables were converted to a ceramic studio in 1990. The entrance is defined by shards of pottery

OPPOSITE: *The talent of both Bonnie and her colleagues at the Ardmore Studio makes a unique contribution to the rich diversity of contemporary South African art and craft.*

LEFT: *Bonnie's* The Nativity *was created for the Standard Bank Young Artist Award in 1990, and was purchased by The Grahamstown Foundation for its collection. Having survived the fire at The 1820 Settlers Monument in Grahamstown in 1994, the bullet-proof glass protecting it shattered under the heat and fragments of glass may still be seen on the charred sculpture today.*

pressed into the cement floor, and a rough, uneven floor extends through the gallery area to work spaces beyond. Rough-hewn cement blocks provide not only the pillars that hold up the old, wrought-iron roof, but also function as partitions. The modellers and painters divide them-selves into distinct groups, and there is a strict hierarchy of painters – determined by themselves – with the best taking up work stations to the front of the studio near Bonnie. Old pictures, posters and magazine clippings of past achievements adorn the walls and three white, electric kilns make loud clicking sounds throughout the day as their temperatures rise or as they cool.

A table with crooked legs holds both fragile, unbaked pieces and the unpainted bisque ware, while the fired, bisque pieces are packed onto a structure of crude pine packing cases to await selection by the painters. The painted pieces are then refired so that the hardened

paint may absorb the glaze better, and the completed pieces are unpacked from the kiln onto the same crooked-legged table. But they never remain there for long as they are coded, priced and displayed for sale, stored as specific orders or put aside as exceptional exhibition pieces. The Studio is visited daily by individual buyers or those who have travelled from distant galleries, and both are anxious to select the best pieces before they are snapped up by equally discerning collectors. The day-to-day chatter reaches a cacophony of sound after Bonnie has shouted *Qoqa* to signal *shayile*, or going-home time, as the artists clear up and the sun slants in through the western windows casting long shadows at the end of the day.

By 1995 it was obvious that the farming operation at Ardmore was not a viable economic enterprise on its own. James Berning had already begun to look for other

opportunities for the family and, as it became clear that the family might move to another farm, Fée began to plan for this eventuality. She had first noticed Mbuse Moses Nqubuka when he was an amiable petrol attendant at a nearby tourist facility and, in February 1995, Fée invited Moses to begin work at Ardmore as the studio manager.

Moses was born in 1968 in Loskop, Maqabaqabeni. His father built traditional thatch houses for neighbours and his mother grew crops and vegetables, before she was widowed and moved her family from place to place before eventually settling at Moyeni. Moses was close to his father and remembers many of the lessons his father taught him: don't trust anyone, think twice before doing anything, and don't believe every promise. Neither Moses nor his two brothers and two sisters were able to go to school, and he started working as a togt labourer on farms around Winterton in 1980. This was followed by

jobs as a horse groom, tractor driver, waiter, receptionist, painter, gardener, and bar steward, but it was not until he became a porter at the Nest Hotel that he began to think about what he would like to do and decided that he had to learn to speak and write English. He taught himself to write Zulu – and English – by repeatedly writing down big words into a notebook so that he would not forget them. By 1994 he had become a petrol attendant, switchboard operator and walking guide at Champagne Sports and, while working here, he got to know Fée Halsted-Berning and the artists at Ardmore. As Bonnie's neighbour, he was introduced to Ardmore and began to paint pieces on his weekends off. Today, as studio manager, Moses has saved enough money to begin building a home at Moyeni. Unmarried, but supporting three children, he enjoys his work but would like to set up a family business because unemployment is so high in the area.

Moses has a responsible job at Ardmore. He has had to learn every aspect of the Studio's operation: packing and firing the kilns, ordering the clay, paints, glazes, brushes and tools, handling orders, organising artists, training apprentices, and paying the monthly wages. His bookkeeping and records must be accurate since artists work for a basic monthly salary and receive a bonus for each piece sold. Since bonuses are affected if works are damaged in the kilns, the technical side of operation is demanding.

In 1996, the Bernings moved to Springvale Farm at Rosetta in the KwaZulu-Natal Midlands, leaving Moses to handle the day-to-day running of the Studio. The move to Springvale diversified activities and some artists followed Fée to the new, smaller version of Ardmore. The Springvale Gallery is situated in a vernacular, greystone shed reminiscent of the stable building at Ardmore, and the creative traditions associated with the Studio now operate at two different rural localities. Fée Halsted-Berning continues to encourage, goad and cajole about forty-five Zulu and Sotho artists, most of whom are women. The Ardmore enterprise has grown to such an extent that Fée spends much of her time planning exhibitions, purchasing materials, and marketing the Studio in both South Africa and abroad.

The driving force behind the Studio, Fée has provided the technical knowledge and expertise, inspiration and encouragement. From the outset, she was adamant that sculptural form is more than a simple pot and, since she speaks little Zulu and most of the artists speak little English, she demonstrates by example. The original impetus for the Ardmore Studio was sculptural but, as the sculptural ceramics became established, decorative functional ware was developed as the Studio's commercial mainstay. The sculptural and functional objects inform each other – an initial idea might form the basis of a sculpture which, in turn, might become the lid for a teapot. The Studio artists follow ideas through different phases and applications and, before they become

OPPOSITE TOP: The plates and other domestic articles are hand painted in the fine decorative technique characteristic of Ardmore.
OPPOSITE BOTTOM: As manager of the studio, Moses Nqubuka is responsible for the artists and the daily functioning of the operation.

repetitive, new concepts are introduced. Fée is quick to praise work that shows effort in its manufacture since the primary aim of the Studio is to combine good form with good surface design, thus creating beautiful objects.

THE ARTISTS AND THEIR ART

When she began working with clay, Bonnie Ntshalintshali made and painted candlesticks and candelabra. Friends and relatives who gathered to watch her at work in the studio started making their own objects and, once Bonnie progressed to the large sculptural ceramics that forged her reputation in the art world, Fée encouraged the other women to create functional objects.

American lead-free paints and transparent glazes were acquired and the different artists began to develop their own creativity and distinguish their work from Bonnie's. Apprentice artists are assessed so that their individual skills may be determined, and they specialise as sculptors or as modellers or painters of decorative, functional ware. The bread-and-butter lines of Ardmore are the hand-built jugs, mugs, butter dishes, teapots, plates and bowls, each of which is beautifully decorated by hand in bold colours and patterns.

The world of the artists is limited to the Winterton district in which Ardmore is situated and, as well as having no formal art training or knowledge of Western or African visual history, most of the artists have a limited education. To locate ideas, they use many illustrated reference books and magazines, drawing inspiration from birds, mammals, reptiles, butterflies and flowers, most of which – even if they are indigenous to the African subcontinent – they have not seen in reality. These visual sources, combined with traditional Zulu folklore, myths and legends, and with Christian narratives of the Old and New Testaments, are transformed to constitute subjects that have become associated with Ardmore. The style is characterised by rhythmic design with sculptural extrusions, exuberant colour and meticulous patterning that go beyond the botanic and animal art of the many

Ardmore imitations that now abound. Clay is so versatile a medium that it permits the interpretation of nearly any object. And so egg cups in the shape of giraffe, zebra and rhinoceros are fanciful representatives of the African plains; teapots transform the farmyard chicken with its tail feathers becoming a useful handle and its open beak the essential spout; fish leap off as the handles of jugs, and lions stand guard atop the lids of butter dishes. Ardmore creates a delightful wonder world.

The artists who produce these enchanting pieces have much in common, but also contribute their own personal life experiences to their work. All have, through the steady income generated by their employment, managed to raise their standard of living. While the artists enjoy their work and gain creative satisfaction from it, the income is the primary source of gratification, enabling them to support themselves and their families.

The founder member of the Ardmore Studio, Bonnie Ntshalintshali was born on Ardmore Farm in 1967. She contracted polio at the age of six and spent four years in Edendale Hospital near Pietermaritzburg with very little chance of survival. But survive she did and, when she returned to her parents, Gwen and Janet, she attended school and learnt to sew, knit and draw. Having reached Standard 8, she left school as her family could no longer afford to keep her there and took piecemeal jobs until she began working at the Studio. When she joined Fée Halsted-Berning in 1985, Bonnie knew nothing about pottery. Her first ceramic piece was a little pig, and she quickly learnt to make small sculptures of animals and birds by studying book illustrations. She modelled and painted the forms and, after a two-year apprenticeship devoted to small functional objects, she began to work on larger sculptures, the subject of which were suggested by biblical stories. Raised without an emphasis on Zulu tradition (although she does like Zulu food), Bonnie is a practising Catholic who attends mass every Sunday, and her obvious familiarity with Christian stories has played a significant role in shaping the iconography of her work.

ABOVE: Although recognised primarily for her sculptures, Bonnie Ntshalintshali is also an enthusiastic decorator of functional pieces which are much sought after.

OPPOSITE: One of the first artists to join the fledgling ceramic art studio in 1989, Punch Shabalala paints delicate and intricate flowers and wildlife.

When Bonnie began to sculpt large-scale pieces, necessity led to invention. To overcome the restrictions posed by a small kiln, Fée and Bonnie found subjects that could be constructed from forms which could be fired separately and then be assembled to create height. The response was encouraging and the new size of Bonnie's work assisted greatly in its acceptance as 'sculpture' by the South African art world.

Bonnie's work and the development of her unique creativity changed her life. She has been able to build a large house and can afford the furniture, clothes and groceries that make her life comfortable. She assists her parents financially and saves for her six-year-old son, Senzo. Senzo's father, a truck driver from Ladysmith, visits Ardmore every two months; but Bonnie discounts the possibility of marriage because, she says, men do not love her, they love her money.

Like Bonnie, Mavis and Punch Shabalala were born on Ardmore. Their father, Peps, was a labourer and tractor driver, and their mother, Lefina, a domestic servant who works in the farmhouse alongside Janet Ntshalintshali. The Shabalalas live on the opposite side of the farm from the Ntshalintshali family and, as they own no livestock, they are not as well-off as their neighbours.

Punch Shabalala, born in 1967 and raised with little Zulu tradition, is a school friend of Bonnie Ntshalintshali. She left school earlier than Bonnie, fell in love and had a child. Since the father was unable to support her and the baby, a difficult time lay ahead – until she came to help her mother at the farmhouse in 1989, and met Fée Halsted-Berning. She started work at the Studio and, taught by Fée and Bonnie to draw animals and birds, Punch became a painter. The design style of her floral and animal motifs is intricate and densely patterned.

BELOW: Mirriam Ngubeni creates her brightly coloured designs from the sources she refers to for inspiration.
RIGHT: Although Phumelele Nene started as a painter at Ardmore, her skills extended to modelling her own pieces.
OPPOSITE: Beauty Ntshalintshali and Beatrice Nyembe work on functional pieces that will be embellished with the sculptural protrusions typical of their work.

Mavis Shabalala was born in 1965, left school in 1986 and did odd jobs on Ardmore Farm before joining her sister, Punch, in the Studio in 1989. Although Mavis does not wear traditional Zulu beadwork, she responds well to the colours and patterns and the influence is discernible in her richly decorative animal designs which also suggest the geometry of West African Kente cloth. Life at Ardmore is, however, not simply a job for Mavis: she believes she has a talent and that she reproduces her experience in her work.

Like the Shabalalas, Mirriam Ngubeni is a painter. She was born in Durban in 1969 and because her mother, Thandiwe, was a domestic servant in Johannesburg, and her father, Sipho, was a farmworker, she was raised by her grandparents in Mangweni Location near Loskop. Mirriam learnt of the Studio from Bonnie and she joined in 1989. She has developed a delicate style that is

applied to humorous bird and flower designs. Unlike a number of the other women artists, Mirriam Ngubeni follows Zulu ritual and tradition, wears beadwork on ceremonial occasions and is *amabhika*, sacrificing animals to her ancestors. Mirriam's ambition is to own her own sewing business in the location and, in order to learn as much as she can from Fée, she followed the Bernings to Springvale Farm in 1996.

Phumelele Nene both models and paints the forms she makes. Born in the Winterton district, she also began her apprenticeship as a painter in the Studio in 1989. Her strongly ornamental style is characterised by solidity and generously harmonious forms, reminiscent of her own stoic nature and the way she handles the severe illness that confines her to her home.

Prominent among those that make the functional domestic ware is Beauty Ntshalintshali (née Shabalala),

sister-in-law to Bonnie. Beauty was born at Maswazini, Winterton, in 1965 and although her father was a farm-worker who once worked on Ardmore Farm, she is not related to Punch and Mavis Shabalala. As a child, she learnt to make *amacansi*, or sleeping mats, with her grandmother and watched over the cattle in the fields. She did not go to school and, as a member of the Zionist Church, does not follow a traditional lifestyle – although, in 1987, she married Andries Ntshalintshali in traditional Zulu custom where a *lobolo* (bridewealth) of eleven cows was exchanged. Andries worked on Ardmore until 1992 when he found work in Johannesburg as a welder, but he returns twice a year to visit his wife and their five children. Beauty joined the Studio in 1988 and was taught to work with clay by Bonnie. She is well known for her hand-coiled and sculpted domestic ware which is much sought after by the painters for decorating.

Beatrice Nyembe is another important modeller: she creates huge jugs, bowls and vases which are then embellished with sculpted animals, birds and flowers. She was born at Mangweni, Estcourt, in 1964 and because her father worked in Johannesburg and her mother was a domestic worker, she was raised by her grandparents in a traditional Zulu household. She came to the Studio in 1988 and chose to build with clay because she thought painting would be difficult. She controls her own earnings and does not support her unemployed husband, Mazibuko, because her main concern is to feed and clothe her five children.

In contrast to the large forms created by Beatrice, Elizabeth Ngubeni creates small, delicate jugs and bowls. She was born in 1956 at KwaVala – over the hill from Ardmore – and, before she came to Ardmore, she made *amacansi* (sleeping mats) and *izicephu* (wedding mats).

RIGHT: *Although she had had no exposure to working with clay prior to joining Ardmore, Elizabeth Ngubeni now produces teacups and jugs which make an important contribution to the Studio's output.*
OPPOSITE LEFT: The strong forms modelled by Sotho artist, Josephine Ghesa, contrast with the exuberantly ornate pieces of the other Ardmore artists.
OPPOSITE RIGHT: In contrast to the hand-coiled items made by most of the other artists, many of the Studio's functional pieces are thrown by Phineas Mweli on a potter's wheel.

She attended school up to Standard 2 and, in 1982, she married Bongani Alson who works in Johannesburg, and returns three times a year to visit Elizabeth and their six children who are being raised in the Zulu tradition.

Of all the artists at the Ardmore Studio, Josephine Ghesa's style is the most individualistic, possibly because she is a Sotho – rather than a Zulu – artist, and possibly because her work draws extensively on her personal and social experience. Born in Thabazeka, Lesotho, in 1958, Josephine was orphaned at a very early age and spent her formative years with her grandparents. Her grandmother was a potter, making *amakhamba* (clay pots) and *ubhodjun* (drinking vessels), and from her the young Josephine learnt to work with clay. She had no formal education and, before she married William Ghesa, she made and sold clay pots. Her husband rejected her when he took another wife and, having to fend for

herself, Josephine left Lesotho in search of work. She picked mealies on a Bergville farm and then she moved to Ladysmith and KwaVala before arriving at Ardmore, poverty stricken and with a baby without any clothing in a blanket on her back.

As a result of her practical experience with clay, Josephine showed an immediate aptitude for sculpture. Her large, robust works modelled in red clay to give them structural strength, have a rather surreal quality. Seemingly unaffected by her colleagues and their own sources of inspiration, she recognises her style as distinct from the work produced by the other women at the Studio. Concerned primarily with shape and form, Josephine is not interested in colouring or decorating her work. Either the natural bisque-fired colour is retained or one of the painters assumes the role of collaborator and decorates the piece.

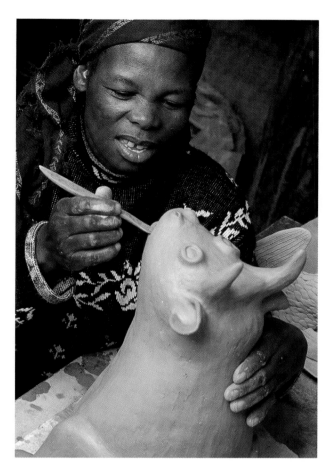

Influenced by Southern Sotho traditions, totems and the religious world of ancestral shades, Josephine's anthropomorphic forms are inspired by her visions; she was visited in her dreams by her grandfather who was a *sangoma*, or diviner. He presented her with gifts of beads and cigarettes to indicate that she too ought to become a *sangoma* but, because she did not want to, Josephine sacrificed a goat to appease her ancestor who has now stopped making demands on her and, instead, watches over her work. Although she discounts the fact that her Sotho traditions or dreams influence her work, she on occasion enthrals her Zulu colleagues with stories of Sotho custom, including references to cannibalism.

Although the example of her grandmother's traditional pottery facilitated Josephine's ability to work with clay, Fée Halsted-Berning directed her sculptural activities and encouraged the development of Josephine's unique vision. She tends to be a loner, isolating herself from the other women at the Studio and preferring to work with her male colleagues. She lives at KwaVala with her two daughters while her four sons, whom she visits annually, live in Lesotho with their father. Although Josephine has been accepted by the local Zulu, she continues to observe BaSotho traditions with regard food, drink and ancestral practices, and she has not yet found a place to build a home.

Josephine refuses to title or explain her works – the pieces are given descriptive titles for the purposes of identification only – and they retain a rather enigmatic and mysterious character. Their strong presence has generated a positive reception from the art world and she has won a number of awards, including the Natal Regional Sculpture prize, awarded only six months after she began working at the Studio.

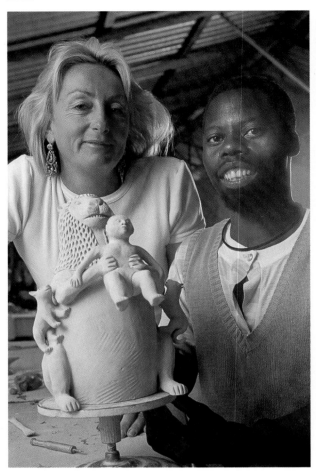

ABOVE LEFT: Nhlanhla Nsundwane is a prolific sculptor and is one of the few artists at the Ardmore Studio who had some knowledge of and experience with clay when he joined.
ABOVE RIGHT: The images that are created by Wonderboy Nxumalo are based largely on personal interpretations of popular imagery.
RIGHT: Although the artists' palette very often reflects a particular period in the development of the Studio, the painters are encouraged to experiment with different shades, which they mix in household items such as ice trays.

The thrown, white clay, functional pieces produced by Ardmore are made by Phineas Mweli who was born in Howick in 1949, one of seven children of Ntuntu and Mbehlunkele Mweli. With only a Standard 3 education, Phineas worked for six years as a builder and painter at Michaelhouse School before he became studio assistant to potter David Walters at Caversham Mill, Balgowan, in 1974. He helped to mix clay, pack kilns and glaze pots, but when Walters sold Caversham in 1987, Phineas had a short spell as a gardener before joining Ardmore in 1990. He accepted the challenge of teaching himself to throw mugs, bowls, teapots, vases, soup tureens and candlesticks and today these products are an intrinsic part of Ardmore's production line stock-in-trade. The potter's wheel used by Phineas was a prize won by Josephine Ghesa and had been gathering dust until Phineas began to work on it. He now also adds his own sculpted elements to these practical pieces before they are handed to his colleagues for painting.

In 1996 Phineas moved with the Berning family to Springvale. His wife lives in Imbali, Pietermaritzburg, and Phineas has taken a loan to buy the Imbali house. His secure income has also enabled him to educate his three children. His eldest daughter, Mpume, is studying Chemical Engineering at the University of Natal, Durban. His other daughter, Nomfundu, is in Standard 9 and his son, Paul, is in Standard 1, and Phineas would like his son to continue his work as a ceramic artist.

Sculptor Nhlanhla Nsundwane is, like Bonnie, a polio victim and, prior to his first job at Ardmore, he relied on his disability pension. Born in 1962 at Engodini, Loskop, Nhlanhla was the son of a migrant railway worker and grew up with his mother and grandparents. His grandfather taught him to model clay animals by the river near the family *umuzi* (homestead) and his grandmother made *amahluzo* (traditional beer strainers). Nhlanhla left school in Standard 1 – when his father became unemployed – and looked after a neighbour's cattle in return for food. He worked on a timber farm between 1984 and 1986

and spent six months as a gardener in Estcourt, before making a meagre wage carving wooden *izingqoko* and *izinkezo* (Zulu meat platters and spoons). Nhlanhla and his wife, Matrina Jiyane, joined Ardmore in 1992, but Matrina left the Studio to have a child in 1994 and died in January 1997 after being struck by lightning.

Nhlanhla's figurative work has been influenced by his exposure to illustrations of Staffordshire portrait figurines, and it is often witty and possessed of an almost childlike innocence. The static forms are beautifully finished and reveal an innate feeling for clay. Although Nhlanhla works at a slow, methodical pace and claims that it took him a long time to learn sculptural techniques, he was awarded the Novice Prize at the Natal Regional Ceramic Exhibition six months after joining Ardmore.

Wonderboy (Thokozani) Nxumalo makes a very individual contribution to Ardmore ceramics through his approach to the decoration of the pre-cast, unglazed, white functional ware that is the main production line of the Studio. He illustrates the plain surfaces with narratives or his own homespun philosophy, using an intaglio etching technique executed in black and white.

Born in Greytown in 1975 and raised on a farm, Wonderboy learnt to read English, Afrikaans and Zulu, and although there was no formal art training at school, he traced and copied the plants he learned about in his science class. His mother's employer – Claudia Khanyile is a domestic worker – noticed Wonderboy's sketchbooks and contacted Fée Halsted-Berning to enquire about work in the Studio. Wonderboy began his apprenticeship in 1994 and, on the strength of the cartoon and movie-based images he had been drawing at school, Fée encouraged him to develop his own style and techniques. He was introduced to the work of renowned Namibian printmaker, John Muafangejo, whose images inspired him. He is also influenced by illustrations of the region's history such as the Anglo-Zulu War, and this study of these illustrations distinguishes his work from the more stylised decoration used by other painters.

In addition to acquiring ceramic skills, Wonderboy also learnt printmaking. Sponsored by the Caversham Press and Educational Trust operated by master print-maker, Malcolm Christian, Wonderboy produces prints which are an ideal medium for his interest in image-text relationships. His printmaking experience has, in turn, suggested ways of decorating ceramics and, having moved with the Bernings to Springvale, he is working on a narrative series of plates and sculptures that relate the story of the death of France's Prince Imperial in the Anglo-Zulu War of 1879.

Wonderboy's use of words – indicating a higher degree of education than most of the other artists – is expressed through designs which incorporate a cartouche or cartoon-like bubble. The messages often express an optimistic philosophy of peace and harmony generated, in part, by the artist's interest in Rastafarian culture. He is not yet married, has no children, does not smoke or drink, and is a vegetarian.

The artists of Ardmore are all distinct individuals who assume responsibility for their productivity. The mutual work environment fosters a cross fertilisation of ideas and influences, and the adoption of particular palettes or forms, at different times. At a time, the use of green and maroon dominated the work and, more recently, a spectrum of dark and light blues, highlighted with yellows and oranges was in vogue. Each piece bears the name of the maker and the painter on the base: *Made by…* and *Painted by…*, and the year in which it was made. In order to confirm the authenticity of the Ardmore signature, a distinctive *a* appears on the base of all originals produced by the Studio since 1997.

Making and decorating ceramic pieces by hand is a time-consuming process. Complex forms may take weeks to model, fire, paint and re-fire. Only then can the artists, and the Studio, see the financial rewards. But the artists are encouraged to avoid formularisation and repetition, and they pursue their individual visions, expressed through their own skills as makers of form and decorators of surfaces. In so doing, each is able to be his or her family's main breadwinner, and develop self-esteem and confidence.

THE COMMERCIAL OPERATION

There were many disadvantages to establishing a studio on a remote, rural, albeit picturesque farm in KwaZulu-Natal. The distance from suppliers of tools and materials, and from sales outlets posed great problems. In addition, the mutual suspicion associated with the traditional farm owner/labourer relationship in South Africa created a human obstacle to initiating a mutually advantageous relationship. In the context of these restraints, Fée Halsted-Berning adopted a number of important strategies. The fundamental consideration was that she could not run the studio as a social upliftment scheme or charity offering handouts to artists and studio workers. Neither could she afford the commission required by commercial galleries. She had to develop a viable business that served the needs of herself and the workers.

She was, however, not alone in wishing to start a rural business. Champagne Valley has changed rather dramatically in the past fifteen years. In the 1980s, this quiet backwater of the Drakensberg provided relaxing holidays for visitors wanting rustic tranquillity and the peace of hiking trails. But the valley has since been transformed by upmarket hotels, a sport centre, time-share complexes and retirement villages. There has also been a proliferation of bed-and-breakfast establishments, craft markets and farmstalls, and the Champagne Valley markets itself as the Mountain Meander, a route offering different experiences for the burgeoning tourist industry.

Ardmore started its commercial existence humbly. Fée and Bonnie painted ducks from a commercial mould, and expanded their range to include farmstyle egg cups and coffee mugs. With the money earned, clay and paint were purchased to sustain the production of functional ware and art objects which are now their signature.

The 1990 Standard Bank Young Artist Award to Fée and Bonnie provided exposure and media attention that set Ardmore apart. Fée used this artistic accolade to market and promote the Studio. She did so by networking. Her friends and relatives in Johannesburg, the art centre of South Africa, agreed to organise house shows of the Studio's wares. Contacts made on these occasions led to more home displays and the formation of a network of Ardmore enthusiasts locally and internationally. Home shows were staged at Meklenberg, a ministerial home on the Groote Schuur Estate in Cape Town, and at the State President's Guest House in Pretoria in 1997. On these occasions, artists from the Studio were present to talk about their work and interact with the art-buying public, a positive experience for all concerned. Thus Fée was able to avoid the flea- and craft markets – the usual arena for ceramics – and bypassed the expenses incurred by exhibiting at commercial galleries.

Selling directly to the public has several advantages. South African and foreign visitors are able to learn about the creative processes involved in Ardmore ceramics, while the artists have developed self confidence and a belief in their creativity and wage-earning capacities.

The commercial operation of the Ardmore Studio is founded on the premise that different people produce different products; some create art pieces and others make functional ware. All have to be paid for their work. The sculptural artists work on an equal-share percentage with the Studio, calculated on the work completed. The formula is applied in a flexible manner as the process of creating sculptural pieces, while not as exacting as that of manufacturing production-line ceramic ware, has its own problems. Some of the sculpture appeals to a niche 'art' market, and some sculptors are very slow workers – and these factors have to be borne in mind in a method of payment that acknowledges both creative input and productivity. The artists could not survive without a retainer, and the Studio therefore supports them until a sale is made at which time they receive a bonus.

Most of the artists at Ardmore work on commission for work they have completed – a practical, incentive-driven commercial strategy. Initially, Fée paid the clay workers for objects when they were taken from the bisque kiln, but she often found herself paying for poorly made forms which were subsequently rejected by the painters, and thus remained incomplete and unsaleable. The painters, working with the best forms, were highly productive and earned more commission. Now pieces are paid for only when they are complete and the maker and painter share the final sale price. The artists thus have a vested interest in maintaining quality control and, as better work commands higher prices, so a culture of excellence has developed.

Artists are also encouraged to be innovative and, for instance, to find ingenious ways of repairing breakages by using glue and a clay fill, followed by repainting and reglazing. Originally, Phineas was responsible for the glaze kiln and if items did not emerge in perfect condition – with a finger mark, for instance – he was blamed for the imperfection, and the sale was delayed until the piece had been reglazed. Phineas, therefore, decided that each painter should be made responsible for glazing his or her own pieces, and this production process resulted in a shared responsibility for quality control, and an increased understanding of the technical issues involved in the manufacture of ceramics.

The painters and makers each receive a percentage of the retail price of a piece on which they have worked, and if they produce a sculpture they receive a bonus. This incentive motivates the artists to be creative and to increase their earnings, with all the benefits that this brings to their families. The artists support large, extended families and are able to finance the school and even, in some cases, the university education of a number of their siblings and children. Many of the artists' children also

OPPOSITE: Prominent in the work of the artists is the flora and fauna of southern Africa, much of which is interpreted from illustrations.
BELOW: True to the signature style of Ardmore, the decorative features of the Studio's ceramics are all finely executed by hand.

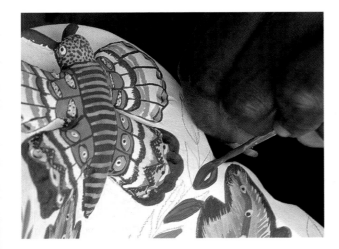

work as apprentices at the Studio on weekends and holidays. They paint less important bisque ware objects which retail at a cheaper price than the main lines, and are thus able to contribute to their own schooling. Education and the improvement of the home environment are the most highly rated indications of economic success, and they determine the motivation of the Studio workers who, if additional income is required in a given month, have the opportunity to earn it through their own increased productivity.

The women in the Ardmore Studio have benefited greatly from the business. Not only do they generate independent incomes, but they have learnt to manage their own money and bank accounts so that they can care effectively for themselves and their children. It is common practice for rural women to have their monthly earnings taken from them by husbands or boyfriends but, since the Ardmore women do not earn a fixed income,

they cannot be controlled as easily by the male head of the homestead. Married women are able to hand over enough of their money to satisfy their husbands, while retaining a degree of control over their own earnings – but many women choose to remain unmarried or live apart from their husbands.

Running a rural business may sound like a romantic proposition but the logistics soon dispel this notion. Great distances must be travelled to get anything done, overheads required to run the Studio are high, and the monthly wage bill is considerable. Fée Halsted-Berning provides all the transport, materials, infrastructural requirements – water, electricity, kilns, equipment, work space, telephone, and fax – and marketing expertise. It has required forbearance and determination to establish the Ardmore Studio in this rural idyll.

Fée sees her main function as selling Ardmore ceramics on a continuous basis as a business. If she is organising an exhibition, she carries the costs of special pieces which are retained until they are exhibited and sold. It takes visual acumen and planning to prepare for an exhibition of the Studio's work: artists have to produce a cross-section of major and minor works of quality, and pieces have to complement each other in design, form and patterning. The Studio struggles to meet popular demand as well as to present showcase exhibitions both in South Africa and internationally, but there is a need to maintain the economic viability of the Studio while attracting new collectors. A unique combination of artistic creativity matched with a degree of economic pragmatism has resulted in the success of the Ardmore Studio.

ARDMORE IN CONTEXT

The Ardmore Ceramic Art Studio was established in 1985 when Bonnie Ntshalintshali joined Fée Halsted-Berning in her small, farm studio. Some thirteen years later the enterprise is a business with both a local and international reputation for producing ceramic sculpture and functional ceramics.

1985 was somewhat of a milestone in South African art: the Second Cape Town Triennial, the Women's Art Festival, and the Tributaries Exhibition all confirmed that South African artists were testing formal and conceptual boundaries, exploring social issues in visual language, and seeking ways of expressing the multi-faceted nature of South African identity. With severe restrictions on free political activity, cultural expression became a vehicle for resistance politics and a means of rejecting outworn Western art formulae. The nature of 'art' and the role of art making in Africa were heatedly debated: change was already in the air a decade before the 1994 elections brought significant political change and democracy to South Africa.

The Ardmore enterprise reflects the processes of change. From the outset, it was a fusion of Western and African beliefs, and responded to social and cultural stimuli. It helped erode long-established ideas about 'art' and 'craft'; it challenged the establishment as represented by the Association of Potters of South Africa (APSA) and South African art galleries and museums, all of which had traditional views on what characterised sculpture, painting, and pottery. Above all, the Ardmore Studio demonstrated that a collective enterprise could change lives and could become financially viable, and it proved that different South Africans could work together for their mutual satisfaction and benefit.

When Fée Halsted-Berning first started submitting her work and that of Bonnie Ntshalintshali to ceramic exhibitions, it was rejected because she did not conform to purist notions of ceramics: she used paint and glue, for instance. Similarly, art galleries were confused about how to respond to work which seemed to be positioned in the craft world. In the end, the art/craft debate was futile in Africa where fusions and cross-cultural references were long established and, as postmodernist theory gained momentum, eclecticism and non-Western aesthetics became acceptable criteria for asserting identities long suppressed by modern purism.

In putting the work of Ardmore into context, it is necessary to state that it is not the only undertaking of this nature that empowered people whose formal education was limited and employment opportunities severely restricted by circumstance. Many urban-based community art schools and rural upliftment schemes are aimed at giving black people the skills which are essential to express their creativity and to earn regular income. Painting, carving, printmaking, embroidery, fabric painting, and appliqué were all seen as ways to produce objects that expressed individual creativity, rendered social comment, and were commercially viable.

Ardmore gradually established its special identity as a studio that produced ceramic sculpture and unique, handcrafted, handpainted functional ware. The products attracted both art and ceramic collectors, and the appeal lay in the unique style of Ardmore: the exuberant rhythms of organic clay forms, the ingenuity with which motifs were combined, the intensity of pattern and colour, and the fusion of narratives and ornamentation.

Drawing their ideas from a huge range of illustrated sources, from artworks and photographs, folklore and legend, imagination and personal observation, the artists of the Ardmore Studio responded without judgement to a wide range of stimuli, and transformed them into painted and glazed clay forms. In so doing, the women and men of Ardmore discovered their own ingenuity, adaptability and resourcefulness. They learnt to work together, and to respect one another's skills. They found job satisfaction, self expression, and both social and economic empowerment.

Fée Halsted-Berning – the driving force behind the enterprise – has had to learn to be artist, teacher, mentor, and business woman. Her energy and vision began and developed Ardmore. Her faith in art, and in people, has reaped exceptional results with far-reaching implications for many families, and given witty, irreverent and beautiful objects to many people who love to look at, and touch, art.

MADE BY BONNIE NTSHALINTSHALI
PAINTED BY BONNIE NTSHALINTSHALI
GOAT POT
1985
33 X 45.5 X 20.5 CM
COLLECTION: DURBAN ART GALLERY
The early animal pots were inspired
by terracotta ducks and guineafowl
planters made in Zimbabwe. They
are both sculptural and functional.

MADE BY BONNIE NTSHALINTSHALI
PAINTED BY BONNIE NTSHALINTSHALI
YELLOW ANIMAL CANDELABRA
1985
34 X 40 X 44 CM
COLLECTION: DURBAN ART GALLERY
The stacking technique added both
height and scale to Bonnie's sculptures.
The animals have holes to accommodate
candles, so they also became functional.
They were painted with Plaka paints and
varnished with thick yacht varnish.

MADE BY BONNIE NTSHALINTSHALI
PAINTED BY BONNIE NTSHALINTSHALI
ENYONI NO ENYOZA
1986
40.5 X 21.5 X 16 CM
COLLECTION: DURBAN ART GALLERY
Inspired by a wooden sculpture by
Zimbabwean Zephania Tshuma, this
is one of Bonnie's first sculptures. It is
purely decorative, and coloured with
Plaka paint and varnish.

MADE BY BONNIE NTSHALINTSHALI
PAINTED BY BONNIE NTSHALINTSHALI
ZEBRA, CROCODILE AND SNAKE
1987
60.5 X 20.5 X 90 CM
COLLECTION: SOUTH AFRICAN NATIONAL
GALLERY
In 1987, Bonnie was still working on
non-religious subjects, and creating
simple, non-narrative sculptures.

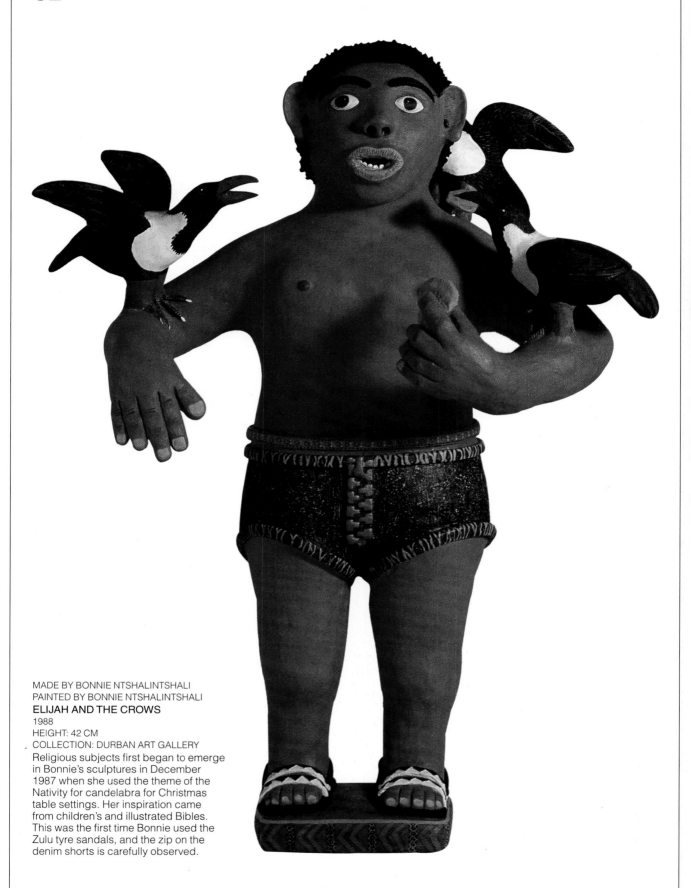

MADE BY BONNIE NTSHALINTSHALI
PAINTED BY BONNIE NTSHALINTSHALI
ELIJAH AND THE CROWS
1988
HEIGHT: 42 CM
COLLECTION: DURBAN ART GALLERY
Religious subjects first began to emerge
in Bonnie's sculptures in December
1987 when she used the theme of the
Nativity for candelabra for Christmas
table settings. Her inspiration came
from children's and illustrated Bibles.
This was the first time Bonnie used the
Zulu tyre sandals, and the zip on the
denim shorts is carefully observed.

MADE BY BONNIE NTSHALINTSHALI
PAINTED BY BONNIE NTSHALINTSHALI
ADAM AND EVE
1990
HEIGHT: 115 CM AND 123 CM
COLLECTION: FÉE HALSTED-BERNING
These two sculptures were created with
separate drums that fit one on top of the
other to facilitate packing and so that
individual sections would fit into the kiln.
The figures, inspired by wooden Yuroba
totems, have been exhibited in Venice,
Rome and Amsterdam.

34

MADE BY BONNIE NTSHALINTSHALI
PAINTED BY BONNIE NTSHALINTSHALI
THE LAST SUPPER
1990
52 X 32 X 55 CM
COLLECTION: STANDARD BANK

The Last Supper was created for the
Standard Bank Young Artist Award
in 1990, and was purchased by the
Standard Bank. Bonnie explained that
there are no forks on the dinner table
because Zulu people do not eat with
forks. The food is served in wooden
platters and Bonnie's favourite drink,
Coca-Cola, is on the table, as is Castle
beer, popcorn, rice and a goat's head.
The figures are solid and they may be
removed from the slab-like plinth. While
the Standard Bank Exhibition was on
tour in 1990, Bonnie had to make two
replacement beer bottles, as viewers
found them so beguiling that they were
broken off and removed.

36

MADE BY BONNIE NTSHALINTSHALI
PAINTED BY BONNIE NTSHALINTSHALI
DANIEL AND THE LIONS
1990
67.7 X 42.6 X 48.5 CM
COLLECTION: PRIVATE
Daniel and the Lions was created for
the Standard Bank Young Artist Award
in 1990, and because Bonnie wanted to
depict more than one lion, she created
a two-headed lion.

MADE BY BONNIE NTSHALINTSHALI
PAINTED BY BONNIE NTSHALINTSHALI
DAVID AND GOLIATH
1990
90.5 X 31.5 X 48.5 CM
COLLECTION: PRIVATE
David and Goliath formed part of the
1990 Standard Bank Young Artist Award.
The figure of David is solid and can be
removed, while Goliath is coiled and
hollow. The Zulu tyre sandals worn by
Goliath were first used by Bonnie
in *Elijah and the Crows* in 1988.

MADE BY BONNIE NTSHALINTSHALI
PAINTED BY BONNIE NTSHALINTSHALI
JONAH AND THE WHALE
1990
60 X 60 X 70 CM
COLLECTION: FÉE HALSTED-BERNING
Jonah and the Whale was also part of
the exhbition for the 1990 Standard Bank
Young Artist Award. The whale is coiled
and hollow, while Jonah is solid and may
be removed from the whale's jaw.

MADE BY BONNIE NTSHALINTSHALI
PAINTED BY BONNIE NTSHALINTSHALI
TRADITIONAL ZULU WEDDING
1991
46 X 37.5 X 27.5 CM
COLLECTION: SOUTH AFRICAN NATIONAL GALLERY
Traditional Zulu Wedding depicts women
in heavy leather skirts and colourful head-
dresses stirring *putu* in big cooking pots.
The blankets are gifts for *lobolo* (dowry).
The dressed-up goat is traditional custom,
and is symbolical at births, weddings and
deaths. The bride and groom are the most
important figures and are depicted much
larger than the cow on the right.

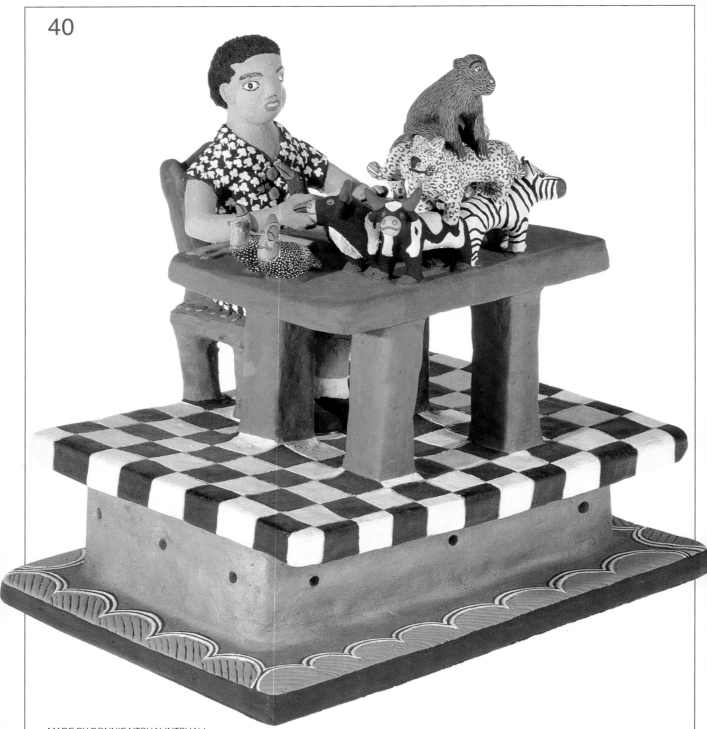

MADE BY BONNIE NTSHALINTSHALI
PAINTED BY BONNIE NTSHALINTSHALI
SELF-PORTRAIT
1991
24 X 26 X 19 CM
COLLECTION: PRIVATE
In 1991 Bonnie was invited by Juliet
Armstrong, Head of the Ceramic
Department, to be a guest artist at the
University of Natal, Pietermaritzburg, so
that she would have the opportunity to
work in a university environment. Bonnie
presented this sculpture of herself at her
work table as a gift to Juliet Armstrong.

MADE BY BONNIE NTSHALINTSHALI
PAINTED BY BONNIE NTSHALINTSHALI
THE WEDDING
1991
18 X 2 CM
COLLECTION: PRIVATE
This piece was created in the same
year as the *Traditional Zulu Wedding*,
when Bonnie was pregnant with her son,
Senzo. Although contrasting in many
ways with tribal custom, this sculpture
combines elements of both a traditional
and contemporary Christian wedding.
The bride, dressed in white, is the most
important character and is much larger
than the rest of the bridal party. The
traditional symbolism is continued in
the goat which bears gifts wrapped
in Western style.

MADE BY BONNIE NTSHALINTSHALI
PAINTED BY BONNIE NTSHALINTSHALI
SANGOMA READING WHITE MAN'S FORTUNE
1993
27.6 X 83 CM
COLLECTION: STANDARD BANK
Bonnie explains that white men often visit
sangomas, and that the farmer depicted
in this sculpture suffered from sexual
problems. Local farmers often consult
with *sangomas* to help solve problems
with Zulu staff.

MADE BY BONNIE NTSHALINTSHALI
PAINTED BY BONNIE NTSHALINTSHALI
APOCALYPSE
1993
75 X 30 CM
COLLECTION: UNIVERSITY OF SOUTH
AFRICA
Bonnie was selected by Bonito Oliva as
one of only eight young artists to exhibit
on the Aperto, or individual section, at
the Venice Biennale in 1993. The theme
was 'apocalypse'. Bonnie depicted God
as a Zulu Chief, warning that 'His people
should stop killing all His animals'. After
Venice, the sculpture was exhibited
in Rome and Amsterdam. The sculpture
consists of separate drums beaded
together with a metal rod through the
middle to hold the pieces in place.

MADE BY BONNIE NTSHALINTSHALI
PAINTED BY BONNIE NTSHALINTSHALI
ANIMAL DISH
1996
58 X 38 X 8 CM
COLLECTION: PRIVATE

MADE BY BEAUTY NTSHALINTSHALI
PAINTED BY BONNIE NTSHALINTSHALI
GENET TEAPOT
1994
32 X 23 CM
COLLECTION: FÉE HALSTED-BERNING

MADE BY BONNIE NTSHALINTSHALI
PAINTED BY BONNIE NTSHALINTSHALI
ANGEL ON THE WHALE
1996-7
15 X 13.5 X 15
COLLECTION: DURBAN ART GALLERY
This piece survived overfiring in the kiln,
where it reached temperatures of more
than 1 300°C. Two other sculptures by
Bonnie were destroyed under these
high temperatures.

MADE BY BEAUTY NTSHALINTSHALI
PAINTED BY BONNIE NTSHALINTSHALI
LEOPARD JUG
1995
54.7 X 20.7 X 45.5 CM
COLLECTION: PRIVATE

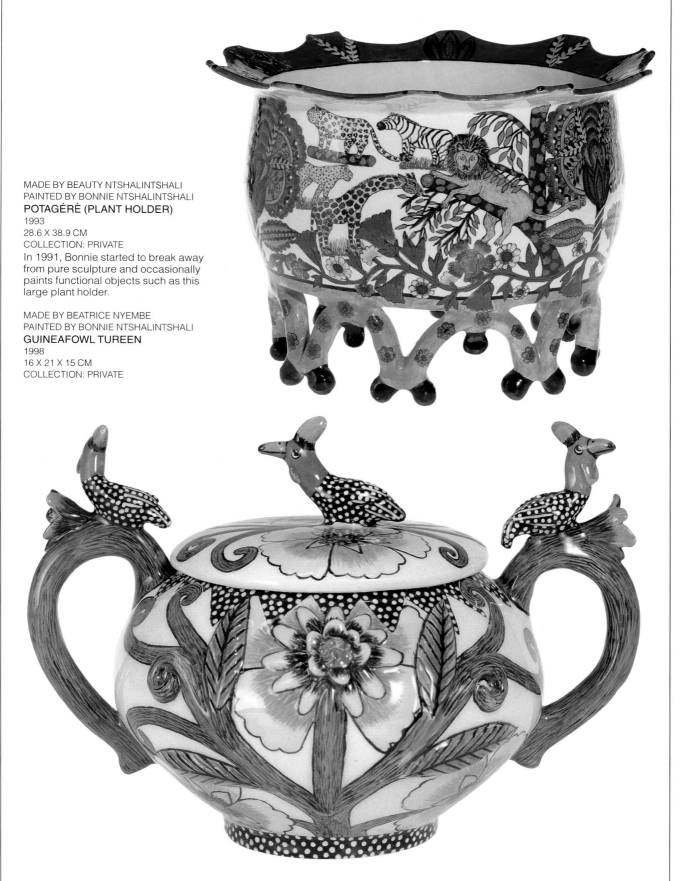

MADE BY BEAUTY NTSHALINTSHALI
PAINTED BY BONNIE NTSHALINTSHALI
POTAGÉRÈ (PLANT HOLDER)
1993
28.6 X 38.9 CM
COLLECTION: PRIVATE
In 1991, Bonnie started to break away
from pure sculpture and occasionally
paints functional objects such as this
large plant holder.

MADE BY BEATRICE NYEMBE
PAINTED BY BONNIE NTSHALINTSHALI
GUINEAFOWL TUREEN
1998
16 X 21 X 15 CM
COLLECTION: PRIVATE

48

MADE BY JOSEPHINE GHESA
TWO DANCING FIGURES
1990
MALE: 52.5 X 36 X 23.5 CM
FEMALE: 51 X 27.5 X 21.5 CM
COLLECTION: PRIVATE
Like Bonnie, Josephine was
initially inspired by the wooden
sculptures of Zimbabwean,
Zephania Tshuma. All Josephine's
sculptures are coiled and hollow inside
and, instead of paint, her sculptures are
finished with boot polish like the traditional
Zulu pots made on the North Coast of
KwaZulu-Natal. Oil paint is rubbed over
the boot polish to give a wood-like effect.

MADE BY JOSEPHINE GHESA
DEVIL AND ROOSTER
1997
45 X 30 CM
COLLECTION: ARDMORE CERAMIC ART STUDIO
In 1998, Josephine was one of 15 of South
Africa's most highly acclaimed ceramic
artists chosen to exhibit at the Long House
in East Hampton, New York.

MADE BY JOSEPHINE GHESA
THREE ANIMAL FIGURES
1993
80 X 38 CM
COLLECTION: FÉE HALSTED-BERNING
This sculpture is one of the few by
Josephine that have a base. The
creatures are half-man half-beast
and their hands form the heads of
other animals.

MADE BY JOSEPHINE GHESA
CHICKENMAN MKIZE
1995
FIGURE: 82.5 X 23.5 CM
OBJECT: 41 X 29.9 X 15.9 CM
COLLECTION: DURBAN ART GALLERY
Chickenman Mkize was an artist who
sold his work outside the Tatham Gallery
in Pietermaritzburg. He was the same
age as Josephine and, when he died in
1995, she chose to depict him with his
road signs and wire-wheeled animals.

MADE BY JOSEPHINE GHESA
JAVUSA
1997
54 X 32 X 49 CM
COLLECTION: SOUTH AFRICAN NATIONAL GALLERY
This is the only sculpture by Josephine which
she has titled, and she explains that Javusa is
a cannibalistic giant. *Javusa* was purchased
by the National Gallery in Cape Town at the
Meklenberg Exhibition.

MADE BY JOSEPHINE GHESA
MAN WITH LIONS
1997
55 X 35 CM
COLLECTION: ARDMORE CERAMIC ART STUDIO
This piece was exhibited as part of the
Down to Earth Exhibition held at the
Long House in East Hampton, New
York, in 1998.

MADE BY NHLANHLA NSUNDWANE
PAINTED BY BONNIE NTSHALINTSHALI
ELEPHANT TEAPOT
1996
31 X 37 X 80 CM
COLLECTION: PRIVATE

MADE BY NHLANHLA NSUNDWANE
PAINTED BY MATRINA JIYANE
MONKEY JUG
1992
27.2 X 12.5 X 28.5 CM
COLLECTION: PRIVATE
Until her death in 1997, Nhlanhla's
wife Matrina Jiyane painted many
of Nhlanhla's pieces.

MADE BY NHLANHLA NSUNDWANE
PAINTED BY MAVIS SHABALALA
SMALL ANIMAL SCULPTURE
1992
33.5 X 17.5 X 12 CM
COLLECTION: PRIVATE
Nhlanhla's earliest sculptures were
reminiscent of Bonnie's early method
of stacking animals.

MADE BY NHLANHLA NSUNDWANE
PAINTED BY PUNCH SHABALALA
PORTRAIT OF FÉE
1995
21 X 18 CM
COLLECTION: FÉE HALSTED-BERNING
In 1995, Nhlanhla was introduced to
Staffordshire figurines which portrayed
Victorian figures, and figures based on
engravings of Shakespearean charac-
ters such as Hamlet, Romeo and Juliet.
In this piece, Nhlanhla has interpreted
his own twentieth-century African version
of Fée Halsted-Berning riding her horse,
Majestic Charm, with her groom, Amos
Shabalala, and her dogs.

MADE BY NHLANHLA NSUNDWANE
PAINTED BY PUNCH SHABALALA
JAMES AND JONATHAN
1995
23 X 25 CM
COLLECTION: FÉE HALSTED-BERNING
Nhlanhla has depicted James Berning
with a rugby cap to show his passion for
the game and a Jersey cow to show his
profession. He is accompanied by his
son Jonathan and his two labradors.

MADE BY NHLANHLA NSUNDWANE
PAINTED BY PUNCH SHABALALA
**CATHERINE AND MEGAN ON THEIR
PONIES COCO AND HALFPENNY**
1995
22 X 18 CM
COLLECTION: FÉE HALSTED-BERNING
The daughters of James and Fée
Berning, Catherine and Megan (with
a dummy in her mouth) are watched
over by Amos, the groom, and are
accompanied by their dogs.

MADE BY NHLANHLA NSUNDWANE
PAINTED BY MAVIS SHABALALA
ZULU WOMAN ON A CROCODILE
1995
16 X 16 X 7 CM
COLLECTION: FÉE HALSTED-BERNING
After Fée Halsted-Berning introduced
Nhlanhla to English Staffordshire and
Doulton figures, he interpreted them in
his own African way, using Zulu figures
with African flora and fauna.

MADE BY NHLANHLA NSUNDWANE
PAINTED BY MAVIS SHABALALA
CANDLESTICK WITH ANIMALS
1995
51 X 18 X 18 CM
COLLECTION: FÉE HALSTED-BERNING
In 1995, Nhlanhla adopted Bonnie's
candlestick idea to add a functional
role to his sculptural pieces.

MADE BY NHLANHLA NSUNDWANE
PAINTED BY MIRRIAM NGUBENI
WOMAN ON BULL
1996
24 X 8 CM
COLLECTION: PRIVATE

MADE BY NHLANHLA NSUNDWANE
PAINTED BY BONNIE NTSHALINTSHALI
IZINDLOVU, AMAKATI NEZINYONI, KUYADLALA
1996
36 X 23 X 11 CM
COLLECTION: FÉE HALSTED-BERNING
Nhlanhla was commissioned
by a client in Durban to create this
piece and is clearly influenced by
Staffordshire mantle vases.

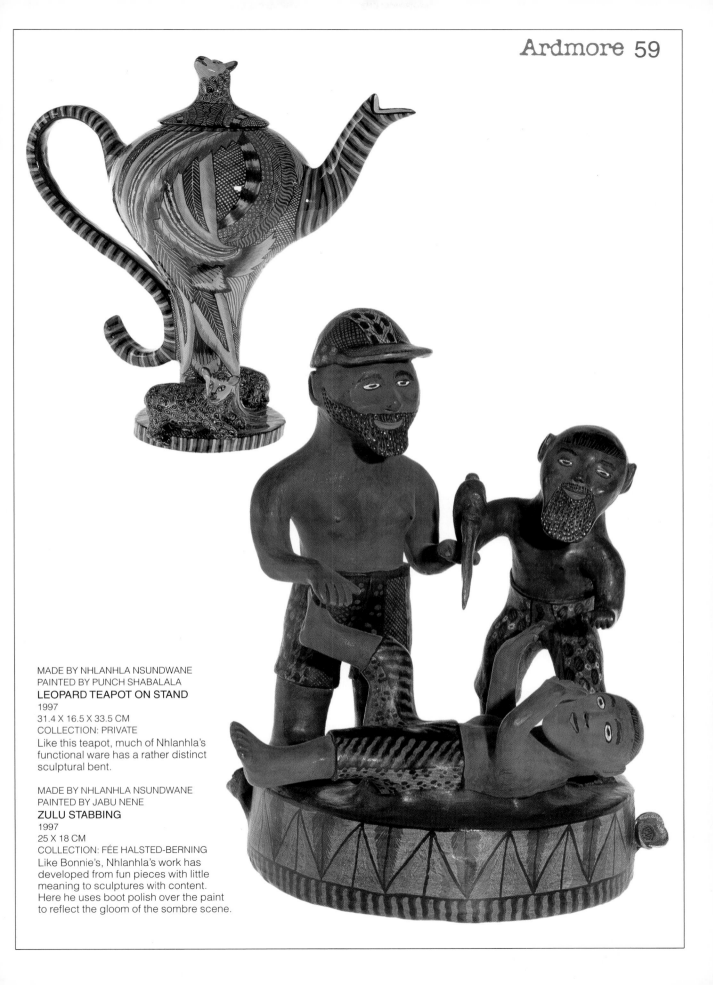

MADE BY NHLANHLA NSUNDWANE
PAINTED BY PUNCH SHABALALA
LEOPARD TEAPOT ON STAND
1997
31.4 X 16.5 X 33.5 CM
COLLECTION: PRIVATE
Like this teapot, much of Nhlanhla's
functional ware has a rather distinct
sculptural bent.

MADE BY NHLANHLA NSUNDWANE
PAINTED BY JABU NENE
ZULU STABBING
1997
25 X 18 CM
COLLECTION: FÉE HALSTED-BERNING
Like Bonnie's, Nhlanhla's work has
developed from fun pieces with little
meaning to sculptures with content.
Here he uses boot polish over the paint
to reflect the gloom of the sombre scene.

MADE BY NHLANHLA NSUNDWANE
(Incomplete)
THE PRINCE IMPERIAL
1998
30 X 43 X 27 CM
COLLECTION: FÉE HALSTED-BERNING
This piece is one of a series depicting
the tragic story of Louis Napoleon who
came out to southern Africa to fight the
Zulu wars on the side of the British. The
prince's party had been ambushed while
having tea near a kraal of Zulu beehive
huts. In this scene Napoleon, in an
attempt to vault onto his terrified horse,
Percy, has fallen under its legs and has
broken his right arm. Trying to shoot
with only his left arm, he was left facing
hundreds of Zulu warriors. The prince
was stabbed in the thigh, but bravely
pulled out the assegai and fought like
a lion to his death.

MADE BY NHLANHLA NSUNDWANE
THE FUNERAL OF LOUIS NAPOLEON
1998
31 X 23 X 34 CM
COLLECTION: FÉE HALSTED-BERNING
This sculpture depicts the tragic end
of Louis Napoleon. The prince's body
was transported from Durban back to
England for a state funeral. Nhlanhla
has depicted the eagles which are
symbolic of the Napoleonic era in the
two far corners of the piece.

MADE BY NHLANHLA NSUNDWANE
**ZULU CALLING MEN TO THE
MOUNTAIN TEAPOT**
1998
37 X 45 X 27 CM
COLLECTION: FÉE HALSTED-BERNING
This teapot depicts a Zulu man blowing
a horn to call men to a meeting on the
mountaintop. Nhlanhla explains that
this is how Zulu men communicate with
others at the foot of the mountain. The
sculptural quality of the work was so
impressive that it was decided that the
teapot would not be painted, but be left
glazed white to retain its beauty.

MADE BY ZEBLON BRILLIANT MSELE
PAINTED BY ZEBLON BRILLIANT MSELE
SOLOMON
1997
39.5 X 36.3 X 28.5 CM
COLLECTION: PRIVATE
Zeblon has created a candlestick with
his sculpture of King Solomon. Like many
of the young artists, Zeblon is inspired by
Bonnie's work, and the plinth is much like
that seen on Bonnie's *The Last Supper*
and *Traditional Zulu Wedding*.

MADE BY ZEBLON BRILLIANT MSELE
PAINTED BY ZEBLON BRILLIANT MSELE
KING AND ANGELS
1998
48 X 45 X 45 CM
COLLECTION: FÉE HALSTED-BERNING
Zeblon Brilliant Msele joined the Studio in
1996 and often uses biblical themes such
as the Creation and Revelation in his work.
He is influenced by Bonnie's early work
and uses Plaka paints on his pieces.

THROWN BY PHINEAS MWELI
PAINTED BY MIRRIAM NGUBENI
THREE COFFEE CUPS
1998
14 X 5 CM
COLLECTION:
FÉE HALSTED-BERNING

THROWN BY PHINEAS MWELI
PAINTED BY MAVIS SHABALALA
CUP AND SAUCER
1998
12 X 16.5 CM
COLLECTION: FÉE HALSTED-BERNING

THROWN BY PHINEAS MWELI
PAINTED BY MIRRIAM NGUBENI
ASSORTED CUPS
1998
COLLECTION: FÉE HALSTED-BERNING
The tea cups and saucers are based
on English styles and the espresso cup
on French designs.

THROWN BY PHINEAS MWELI
PAINTED BY MIRRIAM NGUBENI
COFFEE SET
1998
COLLECTION: FÉE HALSTED-BERNING
Phineas's thrown functional ware are
the mainstay of Ardmore. Buyers on
the European market tend to prefer
the perfect form of thrown objects
over coiled, hand-built pieces, which
are not always symmetrical.

THROWN BY PHINEAS MWELI
PAINTED BY VARIOUS ARDMORE ARTISTS
EGG CUPS
1998
COLLECTION: FÉE HALSTED-BERNING
The popular Ardmore egg cups are
usually painted by the school children
who help pay for their own education by
working at the Studio over weekends
and during the holidays.

MADE BY BEATRICE NYEMBE
PAINTED BY MAVIS SHABALALA
CHAMELEON VASE
1996
13.5 X 15.5 X 14.7 CM
COLLECTION: PRIVATE
The fish vase is reinterpreted here in the
form of chameleons, intensely decorated
by Mavis in her characteristic style.

MADE BY BEATRICE NYEMBE
PAINTED BY MIRRIAM NGUBENI
FISH-BIRD CANDLESTICK
1996
36 X 16 X 11 CM
COLLECTION: FÉE HALSTED-BERNING
In 1996, Ardmore artists were shown
pictures of *The Wally Birds* (tobacco
jars) created by the nineteenth-century
English ceramists, the Martin Brothers,
and these humorous pieces – which
are both functional and sculptural –
influenced some Ardmore pieces.

MADE BY BEATRICE NYEMBE
PAINTED BY PHUMELELE NENE
FISH VASE
1996
36 X 36 X 19 CM
COLLECTION: FÉE HALSTED-BERNING
Also inspired by the nineteenth-century
tobacco jars of the Martin Brothers, the
centre of this piece may be used as
either a vase or a large candleholder.

MADE BY ELIZABETH NGUBENI
PAINTED BY BONNIE NTSHALINTSHALI
BEETLE DISH
1997
7.7 X 47.5 X 33.6 CM
COLLECTION: PRIVATE
In 1997, Fée Halsted-Berning bought
books on beetles and other insects
to help inspire the artists to explore
different subjects. Bonnie deals with
the subject matter in an elegant manner
acceptable to the buying public, but
most clients did not respond well to
the intricate patterns of the theme.

MADE BY AGNES NDLOVU
PAINTED BY JABU NENE
ELEPHANT JUG
1997
43 X 46 X 23 CM
COLLECTION: PRIVATE

MADE BY AGNES NDLOVU
PAINTED BY PHUMELELE NENE
GIRAFFE DISH
1997
9 X 55 X 37 CM
COLLECTION: FÉE HALSTED-BERNING
As seen here, Phumelele – like Bonnie –
paints with a bold, deliberate style and
leaves a considerable amount of white
background to her design.

MADE BY AGNES NDLOVU
PAINTED BY JABU NENE
FISH BOWL
1997
41 X 18 CM
COLLECTION: FÉE HALSTED-BERNING
Inspired by Dutch ceramics, the artists
have learnt to cut out shapes in the clay.
This technique is technically complicated
as cracking often occurs in the kiln.

MADE BY LAYEKI NTSHALINTSHALI
PAINTED BY MAVIS SHABALALA
BEETLE TUREEN
1997
58 X 27 X 26 CM
COLLECTION: FÉE HALSTED-BERNING
This dish was created after the artists
were introduced to the insect theme in
1997. Mavis – like Bonnie – has been
motivated by the insect source material.

THROWN BY MATTHEW STITZLEIN
PAINTED BY BONNIE NTSHALINTSHALI
HOOPOE BOWL
1998
106 X 22 X 76 CM
COLLECTION: FÉE HALSTED-BERNING
Visiting American artist, Matthew Stitzlein,
was requested to adapt an ancient Chinese
peacock bowl to incorporate hoopoes for
Bonnie to paint.

THROWN BY MATTHEW STITZLEIN
PAINTED BY MIRRIAM NGUBENI
ZEBRA TUREEN
1998
27 X 39 X 22 CM
COLLECTION: FÉE HALSTED-BERNING
In June 1997, the American artist
Matthew Stitzlein, accompanied by his
wife Tracey and his brother Nathaniel,
began to train at Ardmore where he
developed a sophisticated style similar
to Phineas Mweli's thrown designs. The
local Zulu artists often work side-by-side
with white artists visiting the Studio.

THROWN BY MATTHEW STITZLEIN
PAINTED BY MIRRIAM NGUBENI
GIRAFFE VASE
1998
42 X 28 X 54 CM
COLLECTION: FÉE HALSTED-BERNING
Thrown especially according to the
Studio's design specifications by Matthew
Stitzlein for Mirriam Ngubeni to paint, this
elegant vase inspired Phineas Mweli's
most recent thrown objets.

THROWN BY MATTHEW STITZLEIN
PAINTED BY MIRRIAM NGUBENI
BUTTER DISH
1998
19 X 25 X 25 CM
COLLECTION: FÉE HALSTED-BERNING

MADE BY PHUMELELE NENE
PAINTED BY PHUMELELE NENE
FISH VASE
1996
41 X 36 X 11 CM
COLLECTION: FÉE HALSTED-BERNING
The mouth of this fish vase lends itself
to a vessel shape and is also inspired
by *The Wally Birds* of the Martin Brothers.

THROWN BY PHINEAS MWELI
PAINTED BY WONDERBOY NXUMALO
SPEECH OF THE SUN AND WORLD
1995
30 X 30 CM
COLLECTION: PRIVATE
Wonderboy often includes examples of
his own poetry on his pieces. This piece
was exhibited as part of the Down to
Earth Exhibition held at the Long House
in East Hampton, New York, in 1998.

MADE BY WONDERBOY NXUMALO
PAINTED BY WONDERBOY NXUMALO
NELSON MANDELA PLATE
1998
35 X 35 CM
COLLECTION: FÉE HALSTED-BERNING
Wonderboy is patriotic and excited
about the future of South Africa and
its people. He sees Nelson Mandela
as a national hero and often uses
Mr Mandela's image as the subject
on large plates.

MADE BY PHINEAS MWELI
PAINTED BY WONDERBOY NXUMALO
**WHY DO THE MONKEYS
ALWAYS SMILING?**
1998
32 X 32 CM
COLLECTION: FÉE HALSTED-BERNING
Wonderboy often relates animals to
people and uses them to illustrate
messages that are important to him.
He carefully contemplates the message
on each piece so that the inscription is
in his best English.

THROWN BY MATTHEW STITZLEIN
PAINTED BY WONDERBOY NXUMALO
BABOON BUTTER DISH
1998
15 X 18 CM
COLLECTION: ARDMORE CERAMIC ART STUDIO
Wonderboy often uses monkeys as a
theme and, on the plate on which the lid
of the butter dish rests, he tells the story
of how baboons learnt to cook mealies
on a fire rather than eat them raw. This
piece was exhibited as part of the Down
to Earth Exhibition held at the Long House
in East Hampton, New York, in 1998.

Ardmore

STOCKISTS

ARDMORE CERAMIC ART e-mail: ardmore@ebucksmail.co.za
KWAZULU NATAL CENTRAL DRAKENSBURG STUDIO Telephone +27 (036) 4681242
ARDMORE SPRINGVALE, ROSETTA Telephone +27 (033) 263767 Incorporating the Bonnie Ntshalintshali Museum

CHARLES GREIG JEWELLERS e-mail: melanie@charlesgreig.co.za Telephone +27 (011) 3254477
JOHANNESBURG SHOP U34 HYDE PARK SHOPPING CENTRE
MICHELANGELO HOTEL SANDTON
THE GRACE HOTEL ROSEBANK
SUN CITY THE PALACE AT THE LOST CITY
CAPE TOWN V&A WATERFRONT

AFRICAN SOUVENIRS e-mail: afrisouv@mweb.co.za Telephone + 27 (021) 4238008.
CAPE TOWN MARKET HOUSE 5 GREEN MARKET SQUARE

GALLERY ON THE SQUARE e-mail: gots@mweb.co.za Telephone + 27 (011) 7842847/8
JOHANNESBURG: SHOP 32 SANDTON SQUARE SANDTON

OTHER SELECTED STOCKISTS: WEBSITE www.ardmoreceramics.co.za

EXHIBITED AND SOLD IN CHRISTIES, LONDON

NEW YORK, BOSTON, FLORIDA, NEW JERSEY, SANTA FE,
AMSTERDAM, VENICE, ROME, PARIS, CANNES, DÜSSELDORF,
HAMBURG, STUTTGART, KUALA LUMPUR.

FERNWOOD PRESS

FERNWOOD PRESS
P O BOX 15344
VLAEBERG 8018
SOUTH AFRICA
WEBSITE www.fernwoodpress.co.za
REGISTRATION NUMBER 90/04463/07

First Published 1998

Reprinted 2003

Copyright © Photographs, 1998 Anthony Bannister: pages 1 to 29,
except for pages 8, 11 and 12 (left) (Kathleen Comfort) and pages
1, 17, 18 (middle), 20, 24 and 26 (Doreen Hemp); Kathleen Comfort:
pages 30 to 80, except for page 32 (Colleen Wafer), pages 34 and 35
(Jean Brundrit), page 41 (Doreen Hemp), and pages 48 (bottom), 52,
77 (top) and 79 (Ronnie Levitan for Peter Visser).

Copyright © Text Gillian Scott, 1998

Design by Willem Jordaan, Hermanus

Edited by Sean Fraser, Cape Town

Production Control by Abdul Latief (Bunny) Gallie, Cape Town

Typesetting by Gerhardt van R ooyen, Cape Town

Reproduction by Unifoto (Pty) Ltd, Cape Town

Printed and bound by Tien Wah Press (Pte) Ltd, Singapore

ISBN 1 874950 39 3